TONE DEVELOP
THROUGH EXTENDED
TECHNIQUES

Revised Edition

ROBERT DICK

MULTIPLE BREATH MUSIC COMPANY

Cover by Sharon Gold

© 1986 by Robert Dick
Library of Congress Number 86-61675

ISBN 0-939407-00-0

For Henry Zlotnik, artist and great teacher, who guided my early development as a musician and taught the essential tradition of the flute and flutists: to learn all one can from the past, to contribute to the present and welcome the future.

ACKNOWLEDGEMENTS

There are many who helped in the gestation of this work. It certainly isn't possible either to form or express ideas about tone development in a vacuum, and I happily acknowledge the many influences that have contributed to my thinking. Foremost, of course, are my teachers: Henry Zlotnik, Julius Baker, James Pappoutsakis and Thomas Nyfenger, each of whom has effected me deeply. Inspiration, too, has come from many outstanding works in the field of flute pedagogy, in particular the books of Marcel Moyse and John Krell's magnificent "Kincaidiana."

I am grateful to my students Ed Bialek, Robert Griffin, Geoffry Kidde and Rod Lakes for their feedback in testing the material of this book and for their many imaginative suggestions. Thanks also go to flutists Alexander Murray and Bernard Goldberg for their encouragement and advice, and to the master flutemakers Eugene Lorello and Albert Cooper for the many hours spent discussing the practical acoustics of the flute.

Lastly, thanks to Evangeline Piperas, Bobby Naughton, Daniel Asia and Randa Kirshbaum and, most especially, Sharon Gold, for their help in preparing the book for publication.

As a composer and performer, Robert Dick is a leading proponent of contemporary music and is known worldwide for his command of extended techniques for flute. His compositions, primarily for solo flute and solo bass flute, convey the musical language he has created through his invention and development of new sounds and techniques. Mr. Dick is the author of *THE OTHER FLUTE: A Performance Manual of Contemporary Techniques, TONE DEVELOPMENT THROUGH EXTENDED TECHNIQUES, FLYING LESSONS: Six Contemporary Concert Etudes (Volumes I and II),* and *CIRCULAR BREATHING FOR THE FLUTIST.* All of Robert Dick's books are published by Multiple Breath Music Company.

Mr. Dick has performed as a solo recitalist throughout the United States, Scandinavia and Europe, and has given masterclasses at universities and conservatories on both continents. These include the Curtis Institute, Manhattan School of Music, Yale University, the Paris Conservatory, the Royal Dutch Conservatory and the Royal Academy of Music in London. As a teacher, he has been widely praised for the effectiveness and originality of his methods, his ability to relate extended techniques to traditional playing, and his capacity to inspire.

Robert Dick's recordings include *The Other Flute,* (GM 2013 Digital) and *Whispers and Landings* (Lumina 003). He has also recorded on CRI and 1750 Arch Records. Mr. Dick has received a National Endowment for the Arts Solo Recitalist Grant, a Pro Musicis Foundation Sponsorship and a New York Foundation for the Arts Fellowship.

Robert Dick was born in New York City and studied the flute with Henry Zlotnik, James Pappoutsakis, Julius Baker and Thomas Nyfenger. After graduation from the High School of Music and Art in New York, he attended Yale University, receiving a B.A. in 1971 and a Masters degree in composition in 1973. He studied composition and electronic music with Robert Morris, Bulant Arel and Jacob Druckman.

TABLE OF CONTENTS

INTRODUCTION

At the present time, many composers and instrumentalists worldwide are becoming increasingly interested in the discovery and development of new instrumental sonorities, and all indications are that this trend is growing into a major branch of composition and performance. This is especially true for music for the flute. Even in relatively conservative compositions written today, it is a rare piece that is not influenced by new sonorities and techniques, including microtones, percussive sounds, whisper and residual tones, glissandi, and a broad range of new tonal colors and articulations. These influences are also heard in the expanding role the flute is playing in improvised music: the classical avant-garde, traditional and new jazz, and popular styles.

Another important—and not well enough known—reason for flutists to work with new sonorities is that this will greatly benefit traditional playing. This work develops the strength, flexibility and sensitivity of the embouchure and breath support, increasing the player's range of color, dynamics and projection. The ear is strengthened, too: one must hear the desired pitch clearly before playing it when familiar fingerings are not used, and quarter-tones and smaller microtones sharpen the sense of pitch as well. There is only one technique that has come into several compositions that has a negative effect on both embouchure and instrument, and this is brass-style buzzing into the embouchure hole. There is some controversy over the use of this technique, but I have always found it desensitizing to the lips and bad for the flute due to the large amounts of moisture that shorten the life of the pads. Buzzing is not recommended, and I ask composers not to use it.

Anyone who can play, for example, the Hindemith "Sonata" is ready to begin this work. For contemporary music, the preferred model of flute is the open-hole flute with a low B footjoint. This model has a large advantage over other types in that the number of possible fingerings is greatly increased by half-holing the open-hole keys and by the longer tube length. This results in an expanded array of multiphonics and extended timbres, and makes glissandi possible. But having a student model instrument should not be a discouragement. Every flute is capable of hundreds of multiphonics, microtones and the like, and students introduced early to these techniques often progress faster in their traditional playing than might usually be expected. Professionals may find themselves choosing different models for different repertoire, a course I recommend for those who prefer the closed-hole flute and/or the low C footjoint for traditional repertoire. It is important to note that composers internationally have assumed the open-hole, low B flute for decades.

To prepare for effective learning of multiphonics, which require an extended range of embouchure positions, blowing angles, and a more complex use of body resonances than do single pitches, the flutist must begin to simultaneously develop the "silent singing" behind the tone, and to strengthen and increase the suppleness of the lips. Thus, the first chapter is devoted to exercises designed to aid the player in producing optimum resonance. These exercises focus first on the role of vocal resonances and "throat tuning", followed by exercises in natural harmonics, bending and whispertones. The second chapter presents exercises in producing single pitches, both diatonic and microtonal, with widely varying timbres and mouth use. Included are timbral trills and several scales that take the flutist to the very extremes of embouchure motion. The third chapter delves into the sonic world of multiphonics. These exercises cover the basic types of intervals available to both open and closed-hole flutes, which range from twelfths to less than the minor second.

It is stressed that this work should be used in a balanced practice regimen covering four main areas — traditional daily studies, (for these can be supplemented but never replaced), new sonorities, etudes, and repertoire. The flutist may either work through this book in order or begin each of the three chapters simultaneously.

We are in a time of growth and change for the flute, a time when limitations, both technical and conceptual, are being left behind. The flute is taking on roles never before imagined, that of a polyphonic instrument, for instance, or that of a quickly changing voice capable of being drum-like one instant, ephemeral the next, then showing surprising power. All aspects of flute playing are therefore effected, and an important goal is for the player to integrate the immense capacities of the instrument into a coherent whole in which all parts support and strengthen one another. New flute playing is the continuation of the life and tradition of the flute and flutists. There is more for us to say than ever before, and the concept of the flute that will never be outmoded is that it is an instrument of expression and beauty.

SIGNS & SYMBOLS

Names of notes:

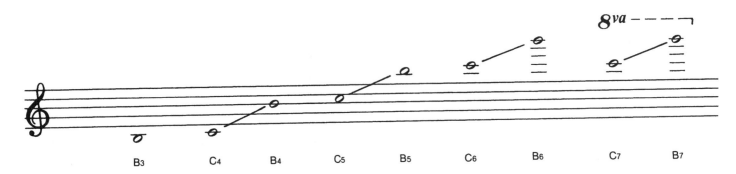

B_3 C_4 B_4 C_5 B_5 C_6 B_6 C_7 B_7

Fingering diagrams:

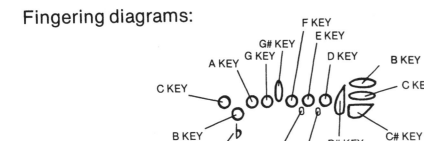

F KEY
G# KEY
E KEY
G KEY
A KEY
D KEY
B KEY
C KEY
C KEY
B KEY
C# KEY
THUMB Bb KEY
D TRILL KEY
D# TRILL KEY
D# KEY

○ — KEY UP

● — KEY DEPRESSED

◐ — OPEN-HOLE KEY WITH RIM DEPRESSED AND CENTER-HOLE OPEN

Intonation:

‡ — QUARTER SHARP

d — QUARTER FLAT

↑ — SLIGHTLY SHARP

↓ — SLIGHTLY FLAT

⇡ — ALMOST ¼ TONE SHARP

⇣ — ALMOST ¼ TONE FLAT

Natural harmonics:

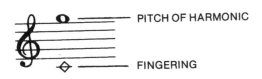

— PITCH OF HARMONIC

— FINGERING

Singing and Playing:

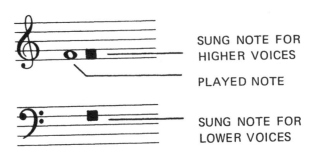

SUNG NOTE FOR HIGHER VOICES

PLAYED NOTE

SUNG NOTE FOR LOWER VOICES

Angle of the flute:

U — NORMAL PLAYING ANGLE

⊂ — TURNED OUT AS FAR AS POSSIBLE

∪ (slanted) — SLIGHTLY TURNED OUT

⊃ — TURNED IN AS FAR AS POSSIBLE

∪ (slanted) — SLIGHTLY TURNED IN

CHAPTER 1

PRELIMINARY STUDIES

THROAT TUNING:
 For maximizing resonance and tone color.

NATURAL HARMONICS:
 For strength of the lips and breath support, accurate placement of the air stream for full and resonant tone, clarification of tone, and development of an alternate fingering and timbral system. This section ends with fingerings and practice suggestions for fourth octave pitches.

BENDING:
 To relax the embouchure, increase flexibility, control of tempering out of tune notes, and use of very wide range of blowing angles.

WHISPER TONES:
 For ability to play without vibrato, practice of very fine focus and placement of the air, small lip motions, practice techniques for third and fourth octaves.

THROAT TUNING

Before beginning to work on tone development, it makes sense to examine just what the tone of the flute is, what factors influence it, and how. Firstly, the tone of the flute is not just the tone made in the instrument, *it is a complex combination of the flutist and the flute*. The sound we hear is that of the air vibrating within the flute, but resonated within the body of the flutist! The tone begins when air is blown across the edge of the embouchure hole, setting up an oscillation of the airstream in and out of the flute, causing the air inside the instrument to vibrate. But the vibrations pass not only forward from the embouchure into the flute, but back through the mouth, neck and chest of the flutist as well. Thus the four primary resonators affecting the tone are the chest, neck (especially the vocal chords), mouth and the flute itself. The sinus cavities are resonators as well, but are considered subsidiary to the main four because their shape, and thus their influence on the sound, cannot be voluntarily controlled. This view of the sound as a combination of resonators allows us to answer the age-old questions: "How can ten flutists play the same flute and sound so different?" and "Why is it that one flutist, playing on ten very different flutes, sounds essentially the same?". This is because the tone is made within the flutist as well as within the flute.

If one looks under the bars of a vibraphone, a resonator tube is found beneath each bar. Each of these tubes is of the correct length to amplify its note, and the throat can function in a similar, but far more sophisticated manner. In order for this to happen, the vocal chords are held in the same position they would be if one were preparing to sing the note about to be played on the flute. To understand this sensation, play a note on the piano or other fixed-pitch instrument that is comfortably in your vocal range. Then, prepare to sing it. Before the note is sung, there is a change in the throat when the vocal chords are brought to the correct position to sing the pitch. When the vocal chords are held in position to sing a given pitch, *the throat is in position to resonate that pitch best*. The vocal range of the flutist, and the octave the flutist's voice is tuned to, do not seem to be critical factors; the accuracy of the pitch, however, is. After all, it really is not possible to tell if a flutist is male or female from a recording. Thus, this technique is equally applicable and effective for all flutists.

Mastery of throat tuning is achieved by practice of singing and of simultaneously singing and playing the flute. Before beginning, it is of critical importance to remember that, unless one is a trained singer, far more air can be put through the flute than can be put through the vocal chords while singing, and that it is possible to strain the vocal chords easily. *When singing and playing together, the air speed is determined by the comfort of the vocal chords at all times!* It is also most important to realize that untrained, or relatively unused vocal chords will almost certainly tire easily, and it is vital to be sensitive to this. While for most flutistic goals a productive practice attitude is: "I know what I want to achieve today, and will stay at work until it is done", the proper attitude for practice of singing and playing is: *"I will practice singing and playing until I feel the first indication that my throat is about to tighten. At that moment, I'll stop, rest five minutes, and return to work on another type of practice"*. At first, only a minute or two a day may be possible. This will build up over time with daily work, and while caution is important, do not avoid this work—it is too important. For those flutists who are reluctant to sing, I stress that singing and flute playing are acoustically so similar that it is imperative to overcome this hesitation and begin. For those who feel that since they may have difficulty matching pitches with the voice, that this means that their hearing is not good, there is much encouragement. Pitch matching, like anything else, involves practice. Many musicians who have excellent hearing cannot control their voices well enough to match pitches well. The ear-voice connection develops through use, and is vital to all aspects of artistic flute playing.

9

The first step for each flutist is to find the lowest note he or she can sing comfortably and *softly* . Most female voices find that this is somewhere in the middle of the octave below the flute. Look for the lowest easy note, one that does not make the throat feel distorted. For many male voices, the octave two octaves below the flute will contain this lowest note. Next, sing the note softly, and while singing, bring the flute up to position, form the embouchure, and bring in the same note in the flute's low octave *while continuing to sing*. This may take a few attempts, but is a coordination soon learned. Now, use that lowest note as the starting point in an exercise similar to that found as number one in Taffanel and Gaubert's daily studies book, but practiced in the following manner:

(This example assumes F♮ as the lowest comfortable note, one octave below the flute for a female voice, two octaves below the flute for a male voice. The actual note is likely to vary for each flutist.)

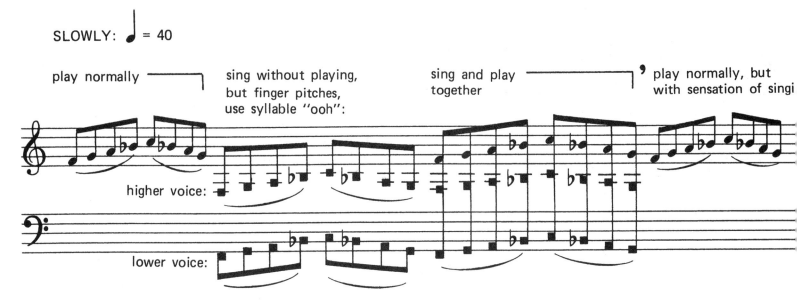

At first, only two or three lines of this exercise a day may be possible, although if the flutist is used to singing, initial endurance will be higher. The amount possible at the start is not relevant. The commitment to the daily work that will result in long-term endurance is crucial.

Since the air's speed will be determined by the vocal chords, and it remains necessary to sing softly regardless of the octave the flute is played in, the embouchure will have to take on an additional role in the flute's second, third and (after much practice) fourth octaves. The analogy that describes this situation is that of a garden hose and wall tap. If the tap is open only very slightly, the water pressure will be quite low, but if the nozzle of the hose is tightened, a small jet of water will emerge at great speed. Singing softly and playing in the higher octaves works exactly the same way. The air speed is low, so that the voice, singing gently, is not strained, but the embouchure is set forward from the normal position for the note being performed, so that a small airstream is squeezed, pressurized at the embouchure so to emerge fast enough to sound the note in the correct octave.

Happily, the "silent singing" created by holding the vocal chords in position to resonate each note takes much less effort than actual singing, and, since the vocal chords do not engage, the air speed is not effected by "silent singing" and it is possible to tune the throat while playing at all dynamic levels, from softest to loudest. As time passes, the daily practice time involving singing can and will expand, as will the flutist's vocal range. Gradually, both higher and lower notes can be added. There will, however, be pitches "out of range" as the practice pattern given above ascends, and when the voice reaches its upper limit, it should be dropped an octave. Upper limit is defined for these purposes as the highest note that can be produced easily, in a relaxed manner, while playing the flute.

After some weeks of work on the scale pattern, it will be time to move on to vocal/flute interval work. While the flute can leap intervals, the voice must glide. Thus, when intervals of a third or more are performed, the voice must leave the first note ahead of the flute so that it may arrive at the second note at its beginning. Practice of patterns like the one below is recommended:

(This example assumes a vocal range of approximately a twelfth, so that vocal intervals are "folded back" when necessary.)

When singing with the flute, use the syllable "Ooh" for middle D♮ down to the low B, and the syllable "Ah" from middle D♯ and above. This applies regardless of the octave the voice is singing in. The third octave of the flute tends to sound like the syllable "Ee", but if this is used behind the third octave notes, they will tend to sound shrill. A discussion of syllables and their effect on tone quality follows later in this section.

If you encounter a "buzzing" sensation while singing and playing that causes the lips to vibrate uncomfortably, almost certainly the cause is too much vocal volume and some degree of inaccuracy of the vocal pitch. To remedy this, immediately reduce the vocal volume by half, then, while singing softly, adjust the vocal pitch until the disturbance stops. When singing and playing causes beats in the sound, each beat represents a one cycle per second difference in pitch between the voice and flute. If you are singing softly enough, these beats will not cause discomfort, and it is possible to eliminate them by truly accurate vocal pitch placement. Also, sing one or two octaves below the flute when possible. Singing in exact unison is the most difficult and the most likely to cause beats.

This type of practice, with the voice in rhythmic unison with the flute for seconds (minor and major), and leading the flute for all larger intervals, should be incorporated into work on etudes and repertoire. Following is an example of vocal/flute practice in the opening phrases of the Bach E♭ Sonata:

This example shows the flute line with several vocal options for higher and lower voices. It is meant to show how each flutist can work out any passage for him or herself.

The effect of mouth resonances is the next area of consideration. Assuming the tone begins with a well-supported breath and properly tuned throat, the syllable that is formed in the mouth will have a profound effect on the quality and character of the sound. As stated before, the central syllables of flute playing are "ooh" from middle D down to the low B, and "ah" from middle D# and above. Artistic playing, however, requires many syllables and combinations of syllables, and selection of these is made according to both technical and aesthetic needs. As a simple way to demonstrate this, play a low C, and, after making sure the vocal chords are tuned to C, vary the syllable formed in the mouth, moving from "ooh" to "aye". A marked increase in the "edge" on the sound, its content of higher overtones will be heard as this is done. In selecting syllables for use in legato passages, *sing the passage* at hand several different ways to find the enunciation that is natural to you. Again, this is a situation where reluctance to sing is counterproductive. Remember that practice is private, and that making mistakes and "missing" are part of the process, best gone through, not avoided.

In specific situations, certain syllables are called for. When tonguing, use of syllables that favor higher overtones, even to the point of nasality, will help the flute to respond faster. Of course, many types of tonguing are used for a variety of articulation. But the most difficult on the flute, and therefore the first to be discussed, is the shortest, clearest tonguing. For this, we need to take a page out of the French school of flute playing and begin by tonguing at the tip of the teeth, placing the tongue very slightly between the teeth so as to block the air, and articulate by withdrawing the tongue. The syllable to be used for this depends on the linguistic knowledge and ability of the player. If the flutist speaks French, then the French "tu" will work well. If the flutist does not speak French, then the syllable can be formed by setting the mouth for "ooh" but saying "ee". Notice how much of the sound is deflected through the nasal cavities. This enhances higher frequencies in the tone, and allows the flute to pick up on those high frequencies. This is translated into faster response and sharper articulation. Once again, be sure to use this syllable with the tongue at the tip of the teeth for single tonguing and the first stroke in double-tonguing. For the seond stroke in double tonguing, the syllable remains the same, mouth set for "ooh" with enunciation of "ee", but with a "k" articulation. The projection of the vocal resonance through the nasal passages is critical on both strokes in double-tonguing. Because so many French syllables involve nasality and placement of the tongue at the front of the mouth, between the teeth, French certainly helps in articulation of the flute, but by analyzing the sonic components of playing, native speakers of every language can play the flute's universal language.

Softer articulation involves modifying this procedure. A range of tone qualities and types of articulation can be created by placing the tongue further back in the mouth and by using syllables of decreasing nasality. The choice should always be determined by the style of music at hand and the expressive desires of the performer.

Lastly, the syllables used in playing intervals can be an important help in their production. When playing a difficult ascending interval, much of the resistance can be removed by changing to a syllable that has more high frequencies in it *before* the upper note of the interval is played. Examples follow:

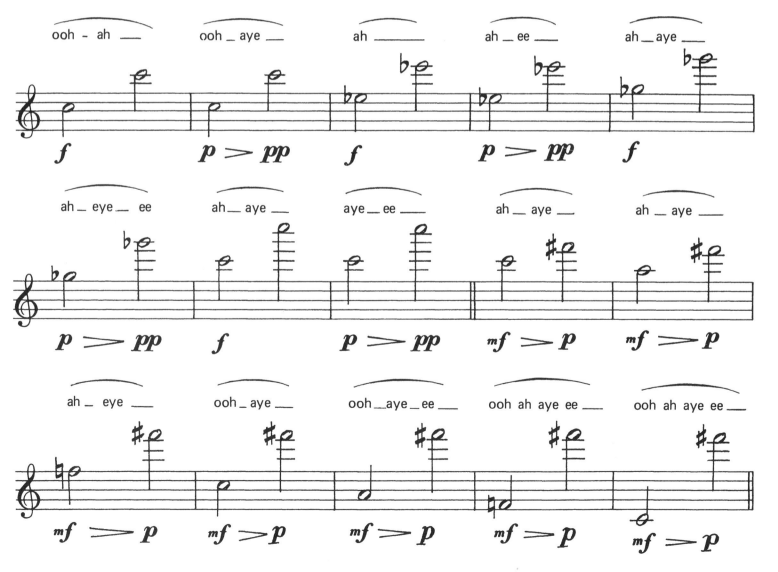

NATURAL HARMONICS

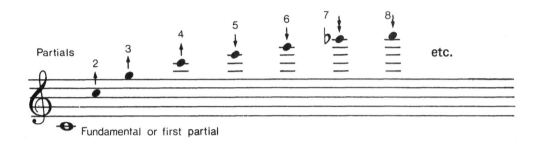

Partials

Fundamental or first partial

When low octave regular fingerings are overblown through their overtone series, the flute produces pitches in the overtone series for pipes open at both ends, called natural harmonics.

Practice of natural harmonics is valuable for increasing the strength of the lips and developing knowledge of the best embouchure position required to produce a full centered sound on each pitch. The art of playing with a beautiful tone, *on and only on,* the purely technical level, can be boiled down to one essential premise: that for every pitch there is an embouchure position (encompassing lips, jaw, mouth cavity and throat) and a shape, direction and speed of the air stream that will, for each individual produce the clearest, "best" resonace.

It has been repeatedly proven that careful practice of natural harmonics improve the tone in normal playing, and the reasons for this are two-fold. Firstly, since the natural harmonics for a given pitch are almost always more difficult to produce than when the regular fingering is used, the lips are strengthened, and this increase in strength may then be turned towards playing with a more relaxed embouchure, giving a more free and relaxed sound. Secondly, the latitude of embouchure position is sharply decreased when natural harmonics are played, and only a good embouchure position will work. Since the best embouchure position for the natural harmonics of a given pitch is also the best for the regular fingerings, the more accurate air placement and focus needed for the natural harmonics develops increased resonance of the tone in normal playing.

As sonorities in themselves, natural harmonics form a distinct timbral system, with each set of partials at a given interval above a fundamental having similar tone color and clear relation in playing characteristics and intonation. As the flutist becomes familiar with the possibilities of harmonic fingerings they should be memorized.

In beginning to practice these studies, the player is cautioned not to overfatigue the lips but to allow strength to develop gradually. It is advisable to omit the highest harmonics at first and to add them over a period of several weeks. In like manner, begin with only about ten minutes daily on the first exercise, and then increasing practice as time passes. Follow practice of natural harmonics immediately with a traditional low register study and/or the bending study found in this chapter. Keep a 2:1 ratio of low tones to practice of natural harmonics, then rest. This procedure is to relax the lips after the strenuous workout that natural harmonics can be, just as a runner walks off the effect of a sprint before resting entirely.

One should avoid the temptation to "dig in" for natural harmonics (or for regular third octave notes for that matter). Instead, think of "reaching out" for them, moving the jaw forward and both pushing forward and turning outwards with the lips. When the embouchure position is good, the air will do the work if it is well supported and focused. The freest sounding natural harmonics are produced without excess effort.

Exercise 1:

This pattern should be played strongly and slowly, giving 2-4 seconds to each note. At first, practice with regular tonguing, then alternate with the "ku" articulation (as found in double tonguing) and with an untongued breath attack — "hu". Do not try to correct the intonation of the partials at first, but rather strive for clarity of attack and accuracy in sounding the desired harmonic with an open free tone. After the player has become familiar with the exercise, intonation should be corrected, as much by air stream and support as possible and with minimal additional lip motion. **

** It can be very helpful to sing each pitch before playing. By doing this, the flutist can insure accurate throat tuning behind the natural harmonics, and can be sure the vowels are correct. Remember, it is the pitch being played that determines the vowel to be used.

Exercise 2:

This exercise involves alteration between the natural harmonics and regular fingering for each pitch. As in the previous exercise slow practice is essential. Repeat each measure three times at *mf* & *ff* and *p*. Similarly, practice with the three articulations — regular tonguing, "k" tonguing and the "hu" articulation — followed by legato work.

Indications for intonation are given in this exercise. The arrows show the tendency of each harmonic and correction should be made in the opposite direction. As these indications are not made in compositions, they are omitted from the rest of the exercises.

This pattern should also be modified and practiced with regular fingerings deleted. Do this slowly at first, maintaining constant intonation, then increase speed until a kind of color tremolo is created on each pitch that has two or more harmonic fingerings.

It may not be possible to play all the way through this exercise at first. Work up to the point where it becomes too difficult; as time passes, the entire pattern will become playable. Likewise, it is extraordinarily difficult to make the pitch corrections for the highest pitches. Correct as much as possible; this work is invaluable in enabling the flutist to correct pitches in traditional repertoire, especially orchestral situations.

Exercise 3:

Practice these scales of like harmonics, the sets of third, fourth, fifth and sixth partials, as one would a traditional chromatic scale study. Working at a variety of speeds and dynamic levels, and adding as many patterns of articulation as can be imagined.

Exercise 4:

This exercise intermixes natural harmonics and regular fingerings in the context of major scales, providing a firm base for intonation. Practice in a similar manner to exercise #3.

Exercise 5:

       This is an "Alberti bass" pattern, in which fundamentals are alternated with their third, fourth, and fifth partials. After practicing at even dynamic levels, mf, ff, mp, and pp, contrast dynamics note to note, as follows:

This exercise should be practiced from ♩=60 to 𝅗𝅥=120 articulated, then legato. Make use of the air speed as the primary means of changing between partials.

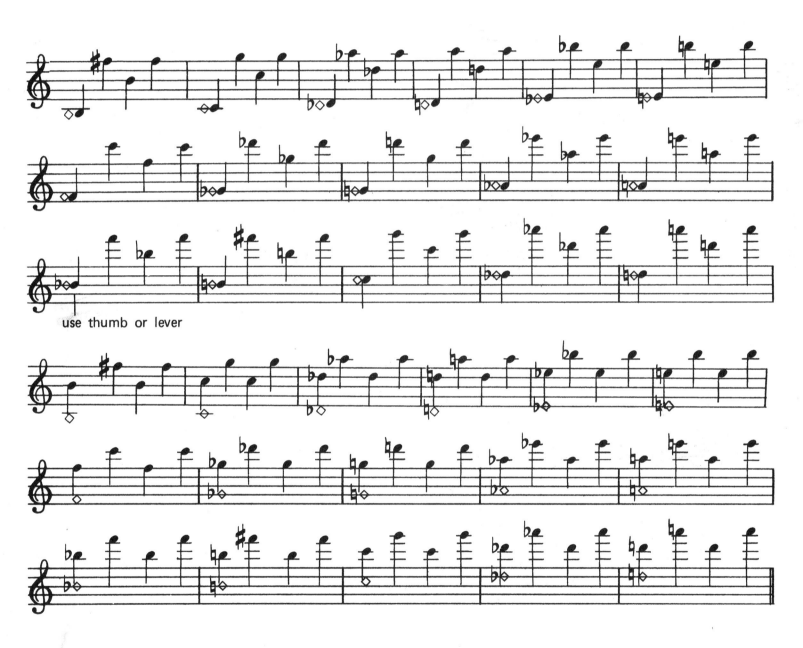

use thumb or lever

19

Exercise 6:
This pattern presents the alternation of the harmonics in broken arpeggios. Work slowly, at about ♩ = 60, using the previously described series of dynamics and articulations.

Exercise 7:

      This is an excerpt from the "Allemande" of the Bach Partita in A minor for flute alone, with natural harmonic fingerings indicated wherever possible. It has been found that if in the course of any piece or etude a narural harmonic fingering is substituted for the regular fingering of a given pitch and that harmonic is missed, then the pitch would not have been sounded with the best possible tone if the regular fingering had been used. For if the natural harmonic is missed, it indicates that the embouchure was slightly out of the best position.

    The Bach example is an excellent vehicle for testing this idea, and after a few alternations between use of the natural harmonics and use of only regular fingerings the piece should sound markedly better than it did at first. This method can be applied to any music, and it is indeed of great value when this is done. When the flutist can freely substitute natural harmonics for regular fingerings at will, without the notation, he or she will be completely at ease in any notated musical situation.

THE FOURTH OCTAVE PITCHES

The range of the flute extends to F♯ above the high C. Composers are increasingly using these pitches, and it is reasonable to say that for at least two decades the professional standard of flute playing has included full technique up to and including high D. With each semitone above the D natural, however, the difficulty of producing these notes radically increases. It makes little sense to begin practicing fourth octave pitches until the harmonic exercises in this chapter have been worked on. The fourth octave pitches require the embouchure strength that the harmonics develop. Because these notes are strenuous, they should be practiced only for a short time, but must be practiced daily if they are to sound good. The benefits of working on these notes are clear: the strength developed will make it easier to play in the third octave even at the softest dynamics and they remove the psychological blocks to the top notes of the third octave, which will not seem so very high. Pitch and color control of the third octave will also be enhanced. The fingerings given below represent the "state of the art" at the time of this writing (1986), and are the result of a continuous inquiry into improved pitch and clarity. Without doubt, further refinements will be made in finding less resistant, but equally good-sounding fingerings.

Practice of fourth octave notes should be done in a ratio of about ten seconds in the first octave for every second in the fourth octave. Following the fingering chart, an example of a practice pattern is given. Based on Taffanel and Gaubert's exercise number 12 on seventh chords, this expanded pattern should be rotated through the Taffanel study at the rate of one key per week until all the notes are established, and then rotated one key per day. For example, the first week, play the expanded pattern on the four B natural seventh chords and play the rest of the exercise as written. The second week, expand the four B♭ chords, etc..

Before playing a fourth octave note for the first time, this procedure is recommended: Be sure the fingering is correct! Check the fingering in a mirror. Then, try the note as a whispertone to find the angle of the airstream. To produce the regular sound, make sure that the jaw is pushed out so the airstream is at a very horizontal trajectory and that the flute is turned out with most (at least three-quarters) of the embouchure hole uncovered. Finally, set the embouchure first, then start the airstream. If these notes are approached with confidence and a sense that they

will be sustained—not played staccato—success is far more probable. Begin at *ff* or *fff*; only after considerable

experience will working at lower dynamic levels be sensible, as, at first, the air itself and not the lips should be doing the most work. The fingerings and exercise pattern follow:

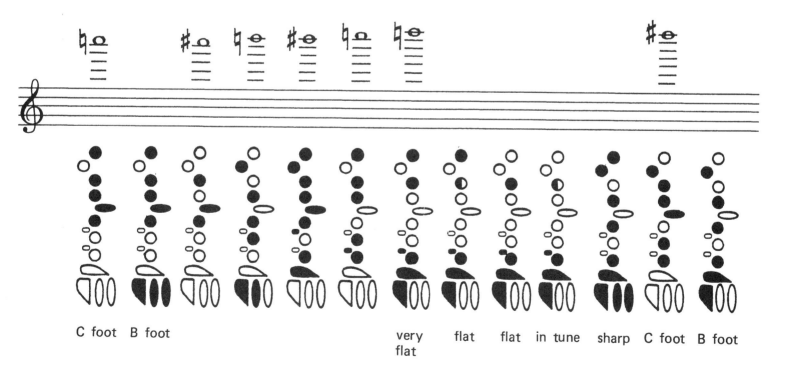

C foot   B foot   very   flat   flat   in tune   sharp   C foot   B foot
                                             flat

Use this pattern for each of the seventh chords in the key to be practiced with expanded range:

BENDING

Bending is the change of pitch without change of fingering. Primarily, bending is produced by rolling the flute in to lower pitch and rolling out to raise pitch. These motions are involved in a much subtler fashion in tempering the out of tune notes in the instrument's scale. To bend a note from correct pitch to as far sharp as possible, usually a quarter-tone, roll the flute out and aim the air very high on the blowing wall, maintaining a focused air stream by pushing the jaw and lips very far forward and increasing the dynamic level until the note is about to break. At the highest part of the bend the tone will diffuse, as the transit distance of the air from lips to blowing wall is unusually long. To bend downwards as far as possible, usually about a semitone, roll the flute inwards, aim the air downwards, pull the jaw and lips far back, and decrease the dynamic level until the note is about to stop. While bending downwards, the timbre changes first to a color somewhat resembling that of wooden flutes, then to a very dark, even smothered quality.

Each pitch is given with its approximate bending range, almost always a quarter-tone up and semitone down. Variations are found, as notes that use shorter tube lengths bend further than do those that have longer tube lengths, and third octave fingerings have a shorter bending range than do notes of the lower two octaves.

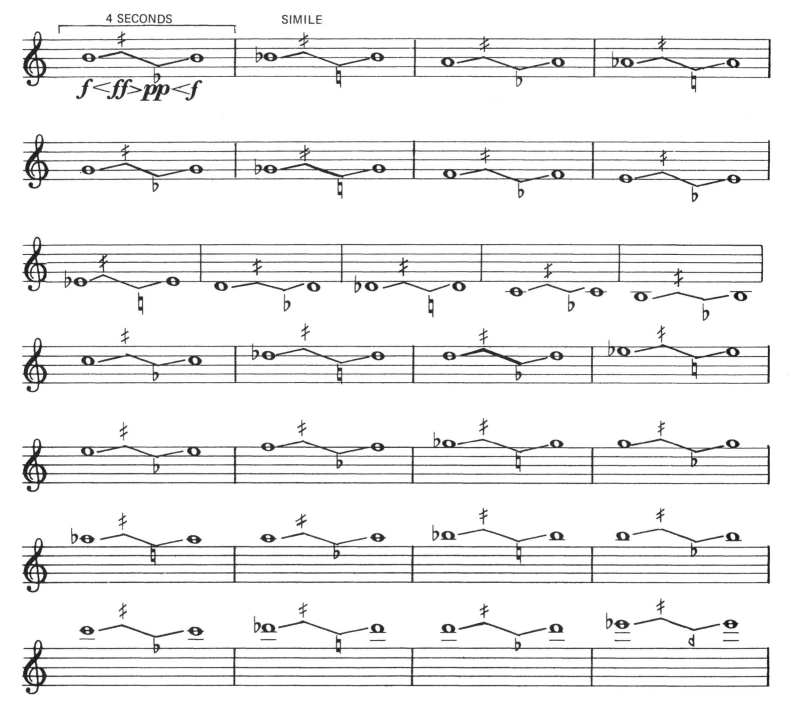

25

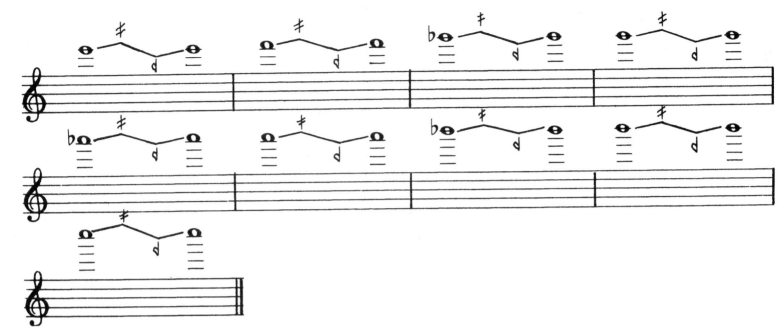

WHISPER TONES

Whisper tones, also called whistle tones and flagolet tones, are produced by blowing in an extremely slow but focused air stream across the edge of the embouchure hole. The air speed is far below that of the softest normally played notes. Whisper tones are the sound of the air breaking over the edge of the blowing wall without exiting the air in the flutes' tube into vibration. The fingering used, however, does have an important effect on the pitch of the whisper tones. It is possible to play every note in the flutes' normal range as a whisper tone, although the difficulty of the first octave whisper tones is very great. Pitches of the third and fourth octave can be more readily played as whisper tones, using their regular fingerings. From low octave fingerings, especially low C (or for flutes with a B foot joint, low B), it is possible to produce up to the sixteenth partial of the overtone series, four octaves above the fundamental.

There are three exercises given in whisper tones, and each will require patient and diligent work. The first involves playing whisper tones in a slow chromatic scale through the third and fourth octaves, up to high F#, using regular fingerings. Tonguing is not advisable at first; each whisper tone should be started with the gentlest puff of air possible. An absolutely steady air stream is needed, as even the slightest fluctuation of speed or angle of the air will result in the whisper tones flipping back and forth between different pitches. At first, the player will probably not be able to produce whisper tones at each pitch given. With practice, the range of whisper tones will increase. A state of controlled relaxation is the key.

The second exercise is a study both of whisper tones and of normally played high notes. It is an "echo" pattern in which a normally played note is followed by a whisper tone of the same pitch and fingering. The embouchure position and air focus that produces the best whisper tone for each pitch will also help produce a free and very good quality high tone when normally blown. Repeat each measure several times, gradually reducing the amount of lip motion between the whisper tone and normally blown note to a minimum. A good way to think of the difference between the whisper tones and normally blown notes is that in the normally played high notes, the air plays a role in supporting the lip opening, while in the whisper tones, the same opening must be made and held open by the lips without any help from the air stream.

The third exercise shows the overtone series for low C (and low B for flutes equipped with it), from the fourth through sixteenth partials. Practice "sweeping" up and down through this range all legato, working to make each whisper tone come out clearly. To produce the highest whisper tones, the lips and jaw should be brought very far forward and the lip opening be the merest possible pinhole. This exercise can be played on any low register fingering, but as the fingerings ascend the range of whisper tones is reduced.

After long practice, it will be found that whisper tones can be played with a light vibrato and can be gently tongued. The flutist should be patient and tenacious, as whisper tones are one of the most difficult sonorities to produce and control, but are well worth the effort for the benefits they yield in ability to play without vibrato and to play at pianissimo levels throughout the flutes' range.

An important aspect of whispertone technique is the position of the tongue. When the tongue is positioned correctly, the loudness of whispertones can be greatly increased, although they always will be a relatively soft sonority. To position the tongue, whistle the note desired, then keep the tongue in the whistle position and play the whispertone.

Exercise 1

Exercise 2

Exercise 3

CHAPTER II

EXTENDED TIMBRES

Many modern compositions ask the flutist to radically change tone color on a single pitch, but often the fingerings needed to do this are left for the player to add. Presented in this chapter are sets of fingerings that yield tone colors of different natures than do the regular fingerings, and these sets should be practiced as scales in themselves and used as a library of alternate fingerings and colors. The sets are:

1. DIFFUSE TONES: Rather "hollow" sounding, lacking in high partials. (some diffuse pitches are slightly flat, but easily correctable.)
2. BRIGHT TONES: Have added high partials and slightly weaker fundamental than regularly fingered pitches.
3. BAMBOO SCALES: Require flute to be turned far outwards, as in highest part of bending tones.
4. TIMBRAL TRILLS: Several color trills are presented for each pitch whenever possible, to give choice of degree of tone color change.

Whenever an unusual angle of the flute is required to play a given pitch, indication is made.

DIFFUSE TONES

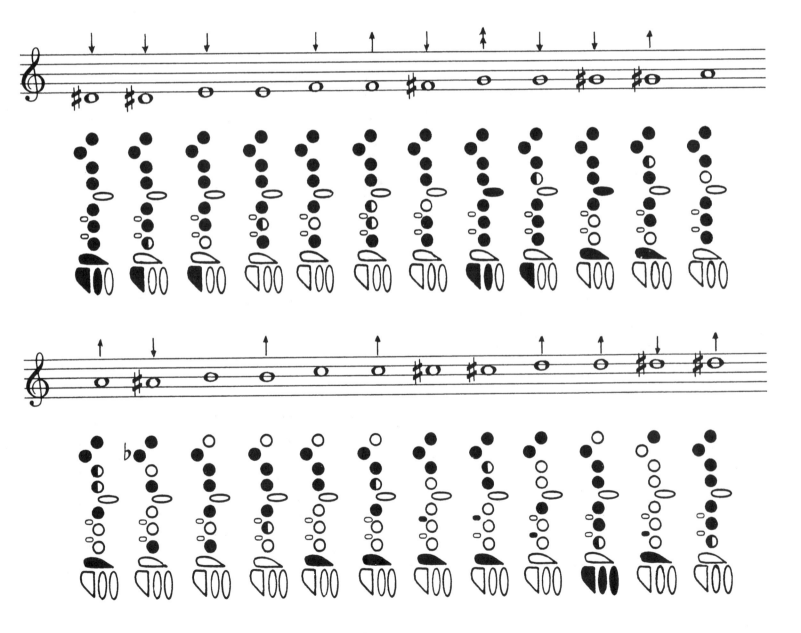

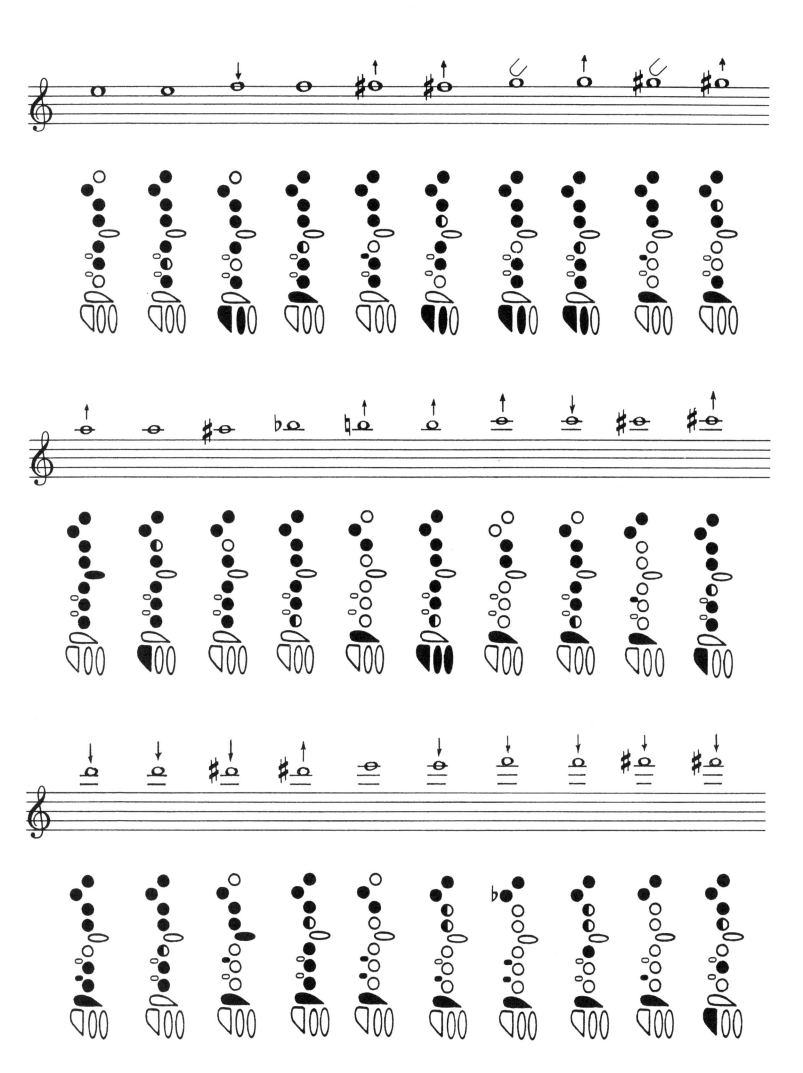

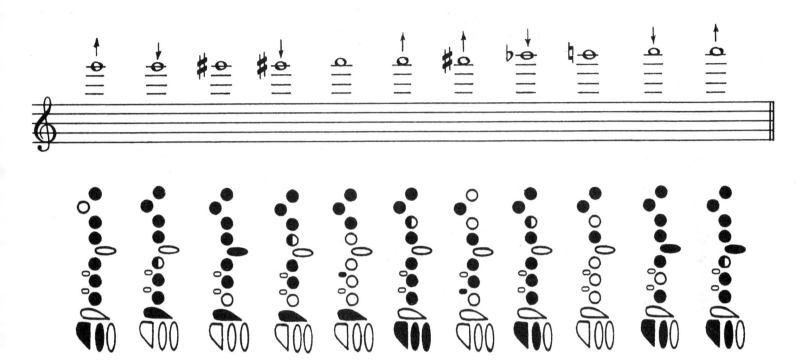

BRIGHT TONES

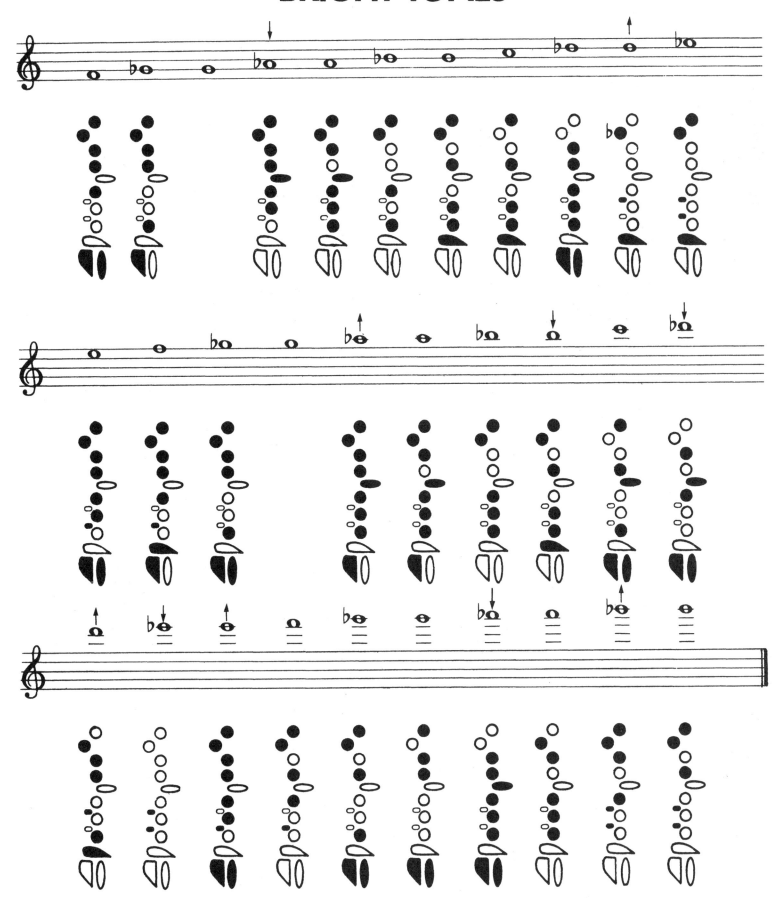

"BAMBOO" SCALES

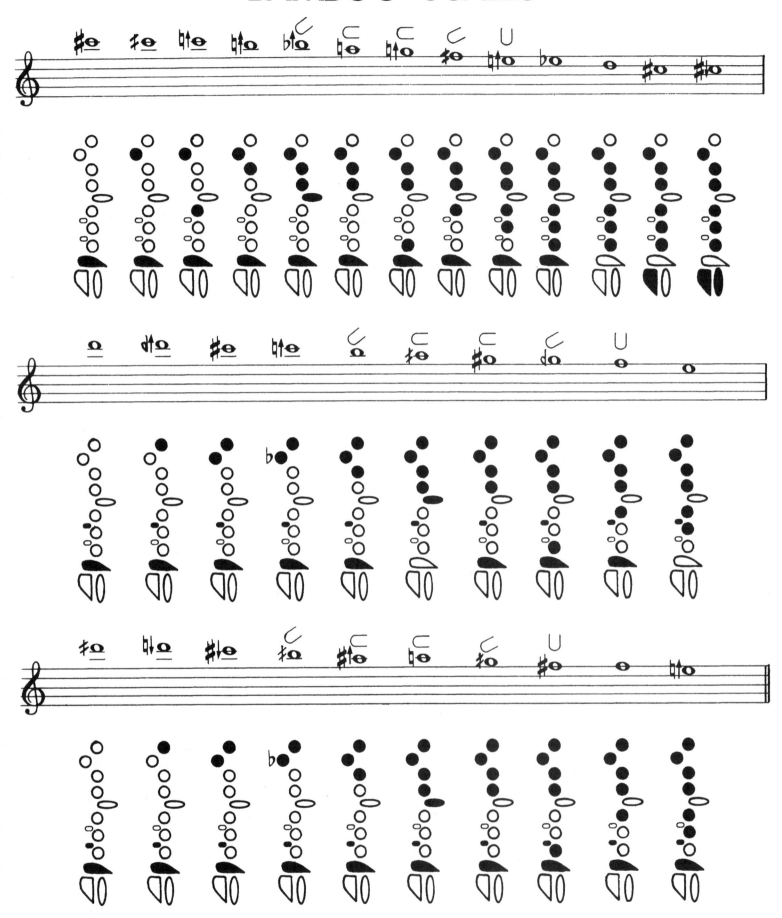

TIMBRAL TRILLS

When more than one trill is given, fingerings are ordered in increasing intensity of color change.

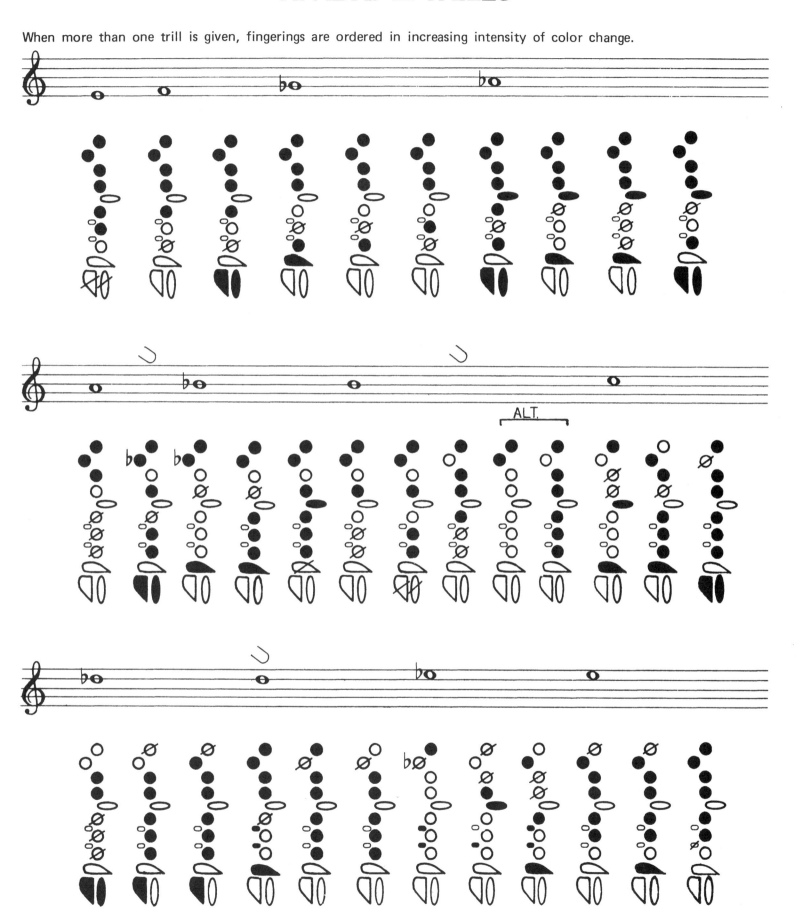

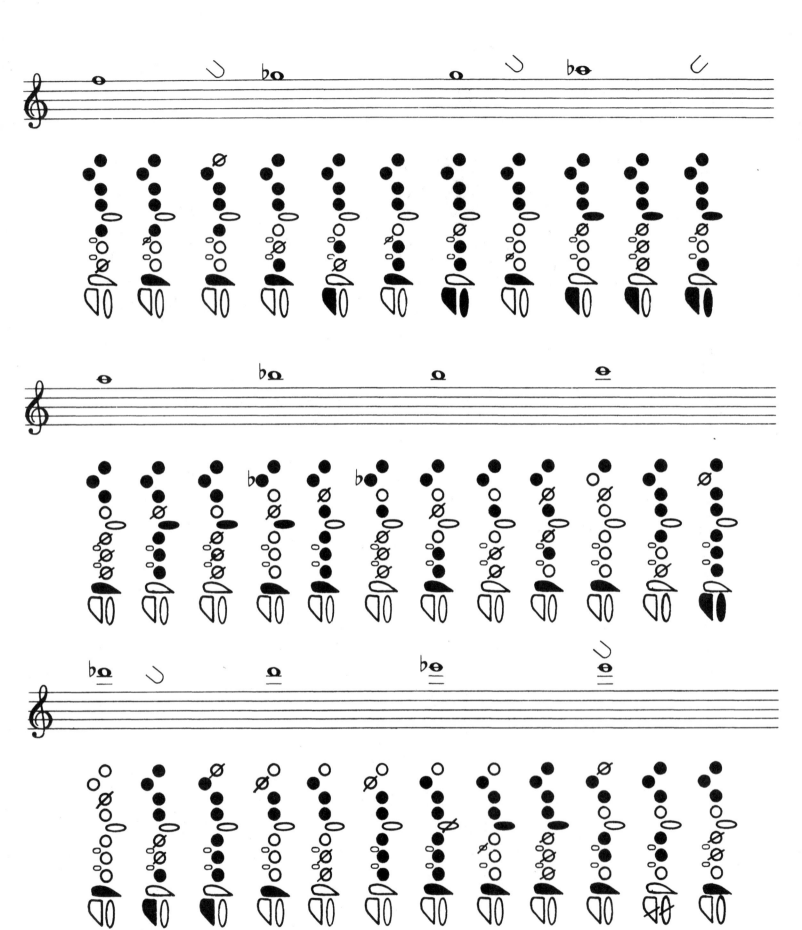

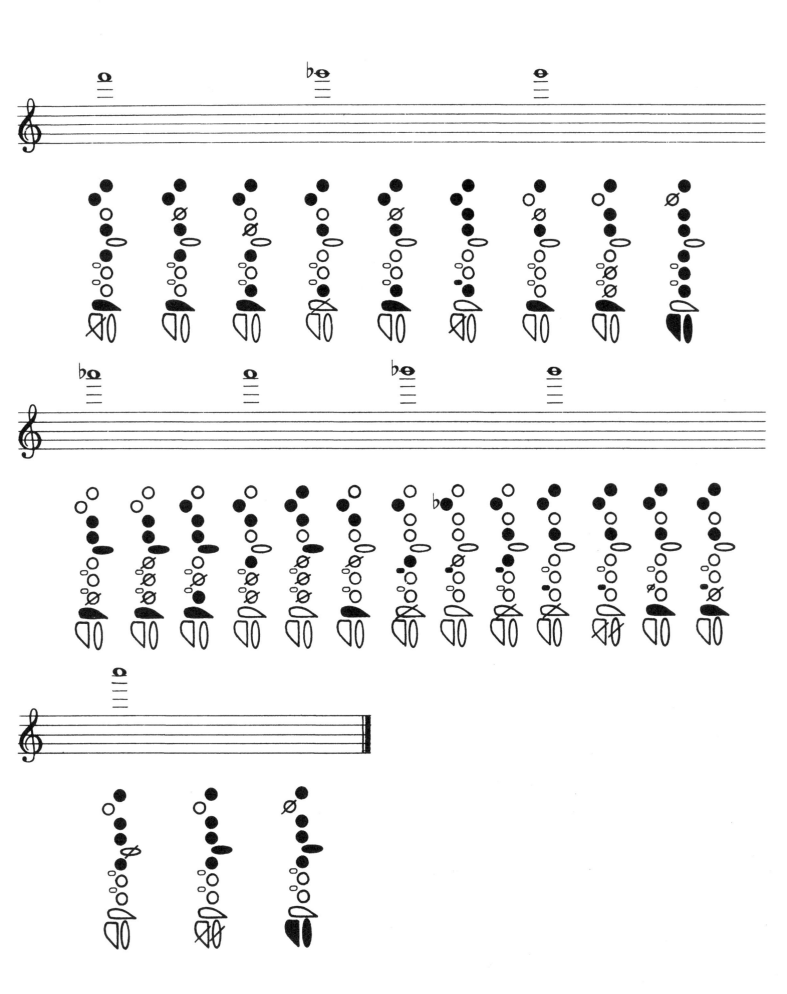

CHAPTER III

MULTIPHONICS

The worlds of multiphonics are the richest new field for flutists. There are literally thousands of possible pitch combinations, ranging from two to five notes together and encompassing a very wide spectrum of intervals and timbres. Some are easily played, others extremely demanding. The interval range of the multiphonics is from less than a semitone to larger than the twelfth, and every fingering, without exception, yields at least one multiphonic, more usually three to six.

The technique of playing multiphonics, also called multiple sonorities, is similar to overblowing natural harmonics, except that the air stream is broadened vertically to reach the target area of each pitch, and the air speed is mediated between the velocities needed to play the notes individually. When learning a double stop, for example, first play the two pitches separately, to become familiar with their target areas and resistances. Explore the dynamic range of the notes alone. Then, while holding the lower pitch, gradually move towards the embouchure position of the highest pitch. During the course of this motion, the two pitches will sound together. Work must then be done towards stabilizing the multiphonic and developing ability in articulating it so that both pitches sound immediately. The most common misconception made by flutists learning to play multiphonics is an attempt to place a "single pitch" air stream between the target areas of a double-stop, rather than use a larger aperture to direct the air to both target areas.

With practice, these embouchure positions and air streams become familiar, and multiphonics can be worked up to the quality expected in traditional playing. The more sophisticated control of the air required by the larger aperture is developed over time, and the flutist is urged to keep in mind the goal of producing multiphonics with high quality sound and not to be discouraged if the multiphonics sound poorly at first. The art is relatively new, and all who study it become beginners again, at least for a short time.

There are six groups of exercises in this chapter. Each presents multiphonics of similar interval content and playing characteristics, which are described in the text heading every set of exercises.

Acquiring a fluid multiphonic technique is a long term process, and a major challenge. But to finally break free of the single note limitation is an important step for the flutist. The wealth of the flutes' multiphonic capacity is extraordinary, and each player will undoubtedly find the types of sonorities that most speak to him or her.

There are two cardinal rules for practicing multiphonics. Observance of these will make reliable production much easier, and will bring the flutist to the level of playing multiphonics beautifully much sooner.

1. After ascertaining the separate dynamic ranges of each pitch, tune the throat to the weaker pitch.
2. Select an air pressure that will work for both notes, and *do not vary that air pressure*. In searching for the correct production of each multiphonic, use the jaw position, angle of the flute and/or embouchure, but not the air pressure.

Exercise B

Exercise C

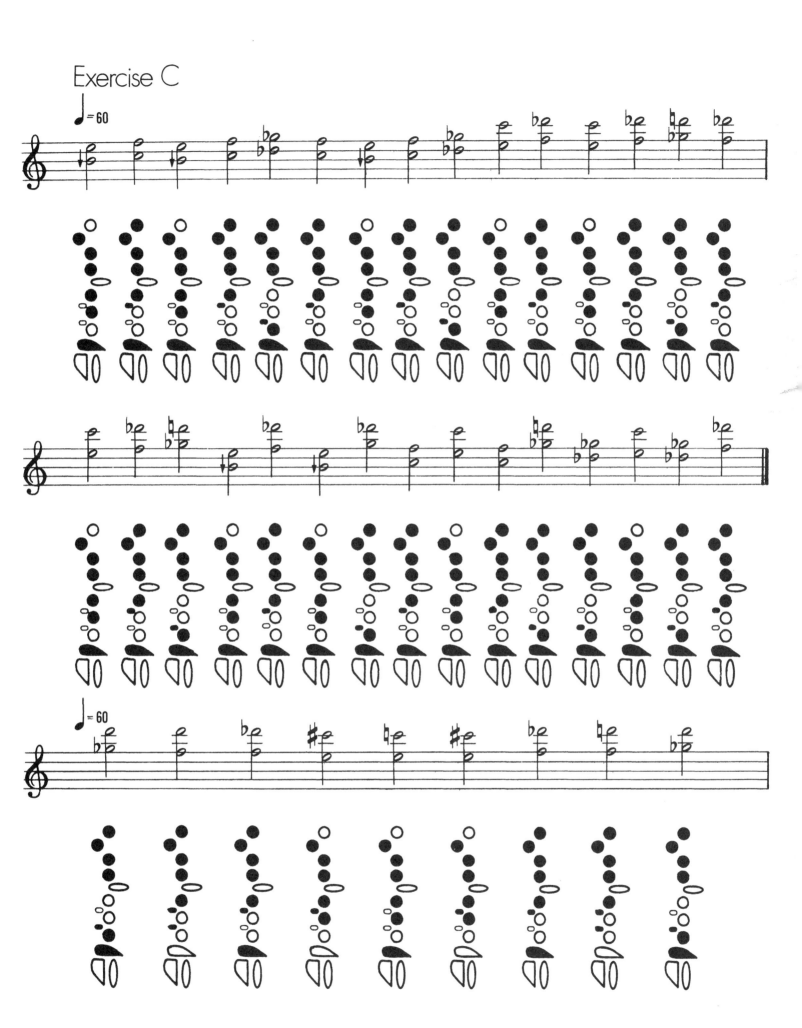

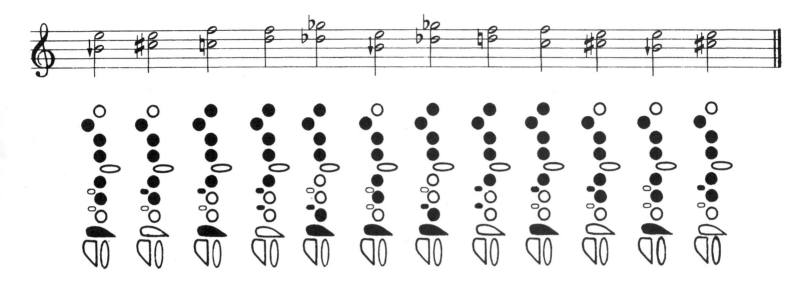

Intervals of and about the major ninth are found in this part, which contains fingerings of a short basic tube length (from Low F4 to B4) vented by a single small hole, again either a trill hole or the C# hole. In the first exercise, begin by practicing each double stop individually, a là exercise A , single pitches first, then together. It will be found that production of the highest pitched intervals will be aided by a slight pulling back of the lips while maintaining the forward position of the jaw. Conversely, the lowest pitched intervals will sound most readily if the lips are brought forward while the jaw drops and moves back. Following separate practice of each multiphonic practice the patterns in rhythm, giving about two seconds apiece to the double stops in exercise D & E. Work towards playing at a solid forte.

Exercise D

𝅝 = 60

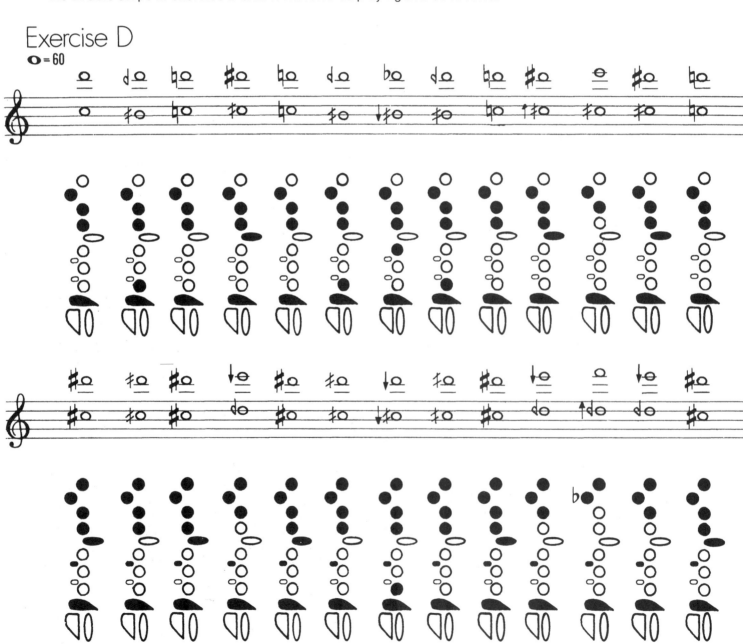

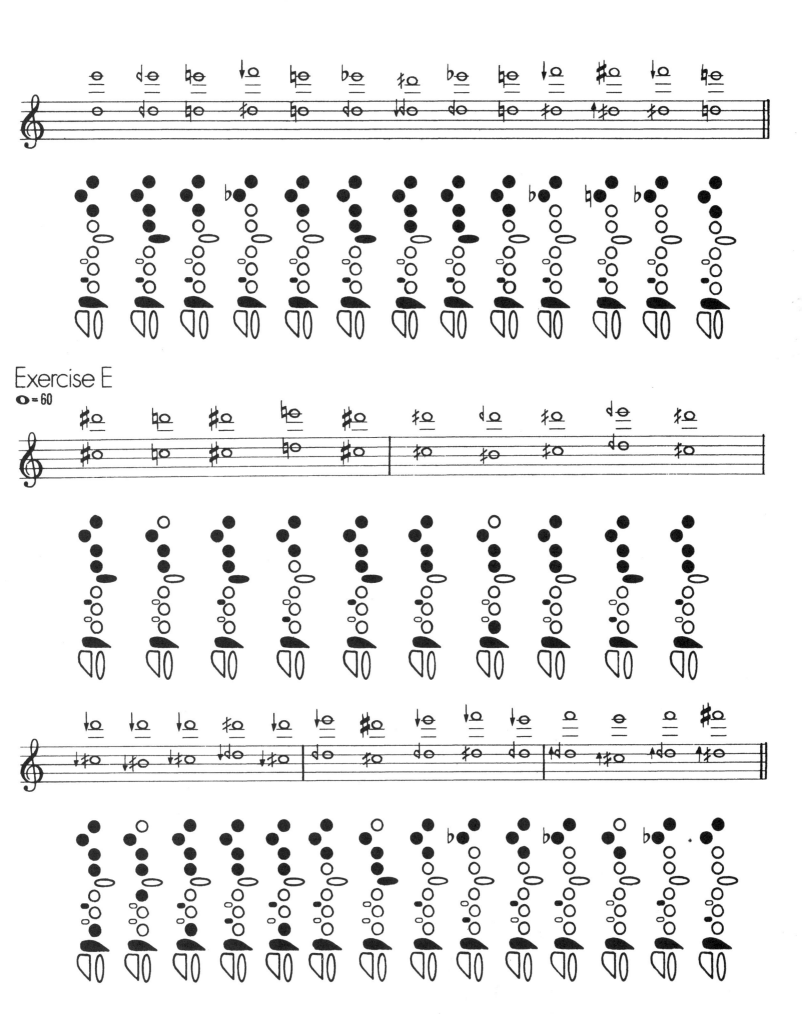

Exercise E

♩ = 60

Exercise F presents multiphonics that use small-hole venting by means of half-hole technique on the open-hole keys. When first trying these fingerings, do so using a mirror to be sure that *the entire center-hole is open with no obstruction of the air by the finger.* "Shading" the center-hole will flatten the pitches and make production much more difficult. It is best to curve the fingers when half-holing as this prevents tension in the hands and forearms.

Practice these multiphonics similarly to those in previous exercises, starting at ♩ = 60, then working faster.

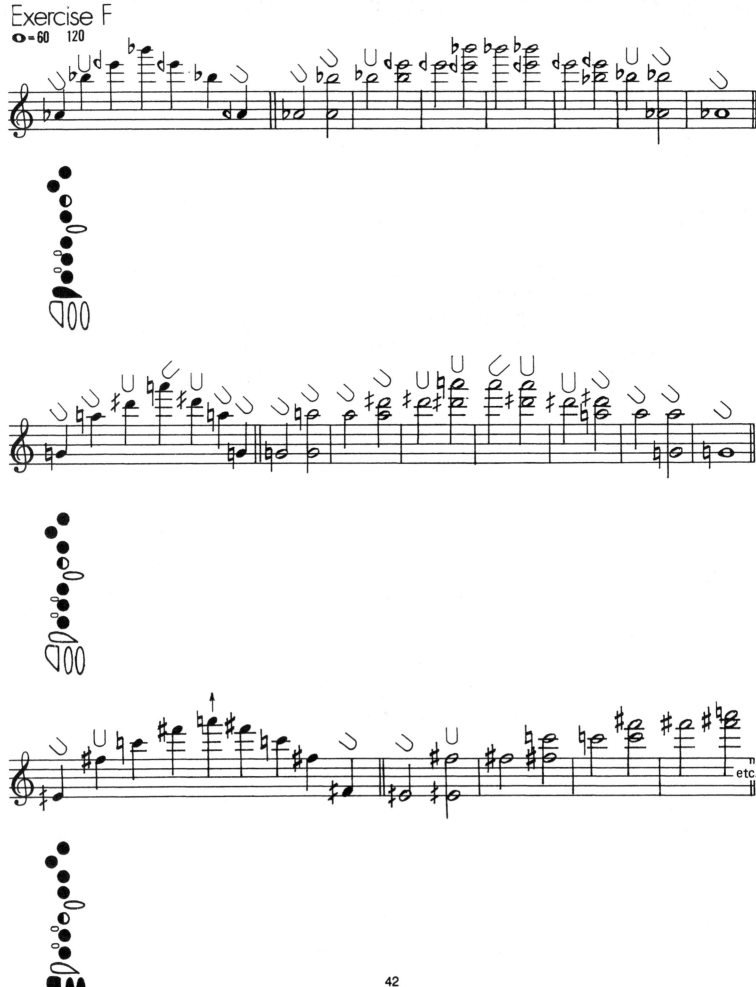

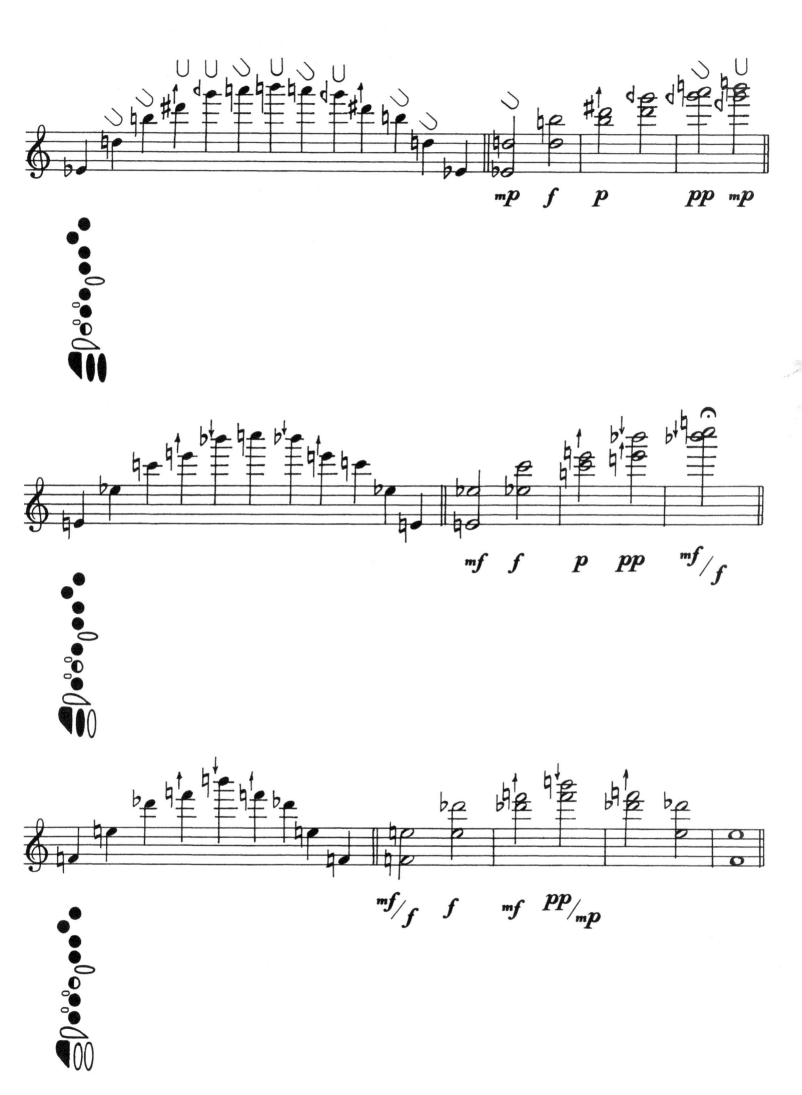

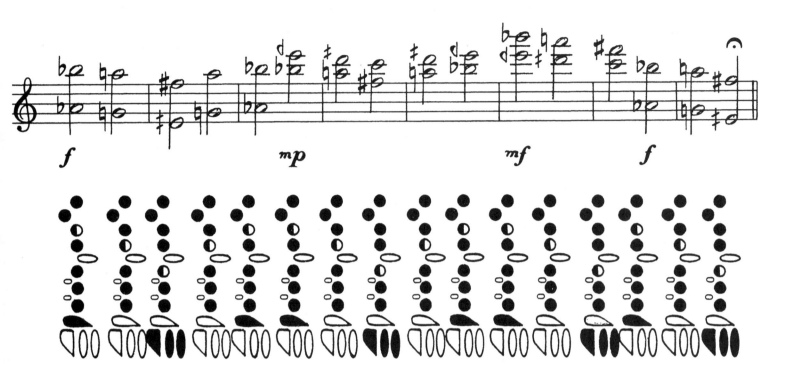

This pair of exercises deals with octaves, first from natural harmonic fingerings, then from alternate fingerings. Exercise G should be practiced at $\sum$ = 72 with the "hu" articulation, then tongued, finally legato. Should the upper pitch of the octaves sound flat, it is usually an indication that the flute is turned inwards a bit too far and is placed slightly too high on the chin. Very clear, violin like octaves are possible and can be freely played at all dynamic levels. Practice from *f* to *pp*, then up to *ff*. As control over the natural harmonics is gained, experimentation in the balancing of the two pitches in each octave interval will prove fruitful. A wide range of tonal colors will be heard and the flutist can make good use of these throughout traditional playing. When doing this work, start on the lower pitch of a given octave, and bring in the higher note as slowly and gradually as possible, striving to glide from single pitch to multiphonic. This procedure is more difficult to play in reverse, from high to low but is splendid exercise for the lips.

In exercise H the intonation of the octaves is very slightly imperfect, thus many of these intervals have a slight bubbly sound caused by the beating of the almost in tune octaves. Experimentation with the angle of the flute will result in the beats changing speed as pitch varies. Start with practice of the double-stops individually, then work up the speed from approximately one second per multiphonic to twice that tempo.

Exercise G

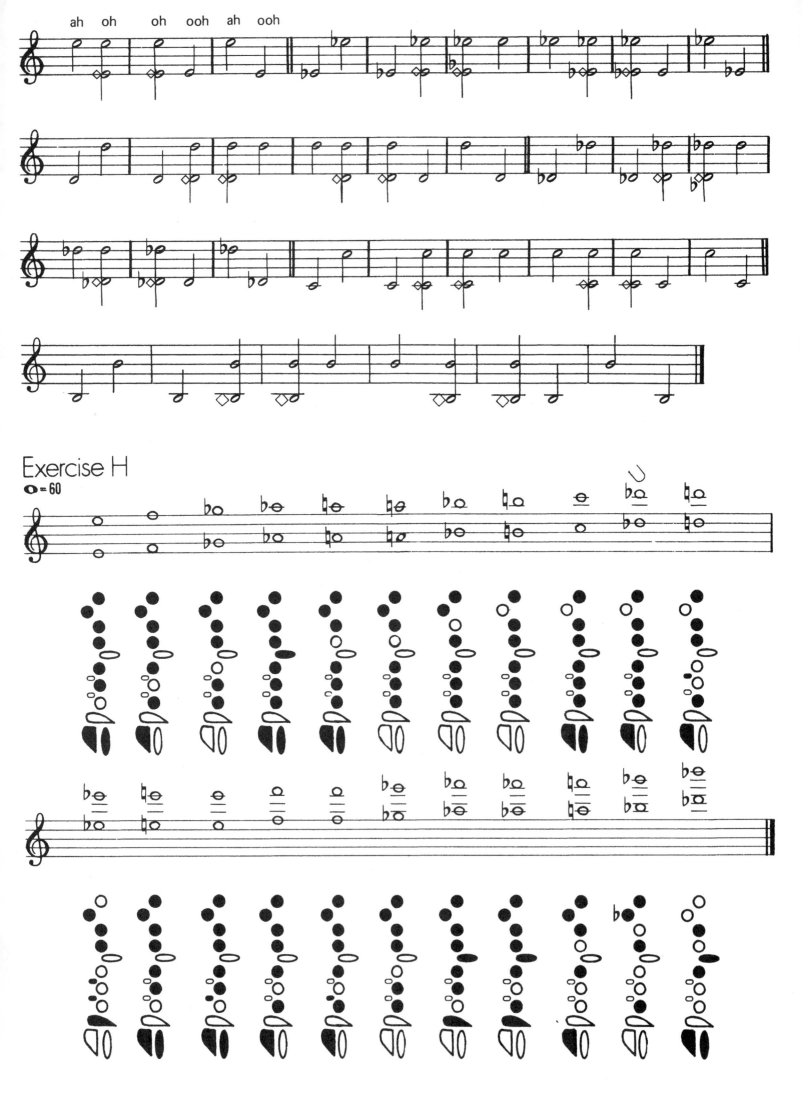

Exercise H

♩ = 60

46

The first exercise involving natural harmonic fifths, is rather difficult. Practice it in the same manner as the natural harmonic octaves. Breath support is critical to avoid smothering the sound. The diamond note head at the beginning of each five measure group is the only fingering to be used throughout the group.

There may be a tendency to turn the flute in to make these intervals easier, but a loss of quality will result. Due to the taper of the flutes' headjoint, the fifths produced from fundamentals from G4 on upwards become progressively more out of tune, first beating slightly, finally becoming quite grainy on the highest fifths. There is only a limited range of correction of these intervals for both pitches move in an almost identically manner when tempering is made. These highest fifths are very strenuous to practice, and should be added gradually into daily work.

Exercise J combines natural harmonic octaves and fifths in a "common tone" exercise. The diamond note head at the start of each measure is the only fingering to be used throughout the measure. This exercise provides a good framework for intonation, as the upper note of each octave and the lower of each fifth generated by the same fingering should be identical in pitch. First work with articulations — "hu", regular tonguing and "k" tonguing, then legato. ♩ = 60-90, then *mf* to *f*.

Exercise K combines previous materials: natural harmonic octaves, alternately fingered and natural harmonic fifths.

Exercise I

Exercise J

○ = 60 - 90

These multiphonics have a seemingly paradoxical intervalic structure: a very small interval as the lowest multiphonic followed by a repetition of that interval at the octave, sometimes with slight pitch change, usually not. Follow the indications for the angle of the flute carefully and work at very low dynamic levels, except for intervals that require that the flute be turned out radically. A rock steady air stream, without any vibrato at all, is needed to play the intervals that are played with the flute turned inwards. These sonorities are delicate, and will help the player to develop very fine control of the focus and direction of the air stream. Exercise L presents the pitches and intervals yielded by each fingering and these multiphonics are inter-mixed in exercise M

$\quad$ = 40 - 60 *pp* to *p*.

Exercise L
VERY SLOWLY

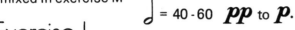

50

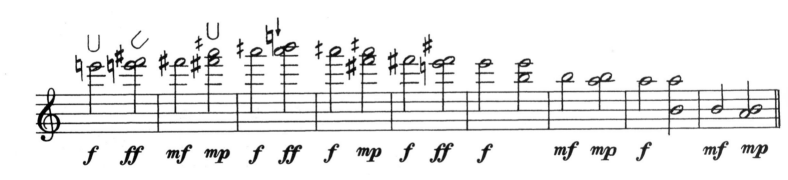

mf   *mp*

mp   *p*

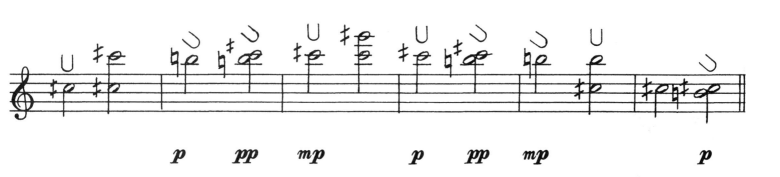

p   *pp*   *mp*   *p*   *pp*   *mp*   *p*

Exercise M

♩= 60

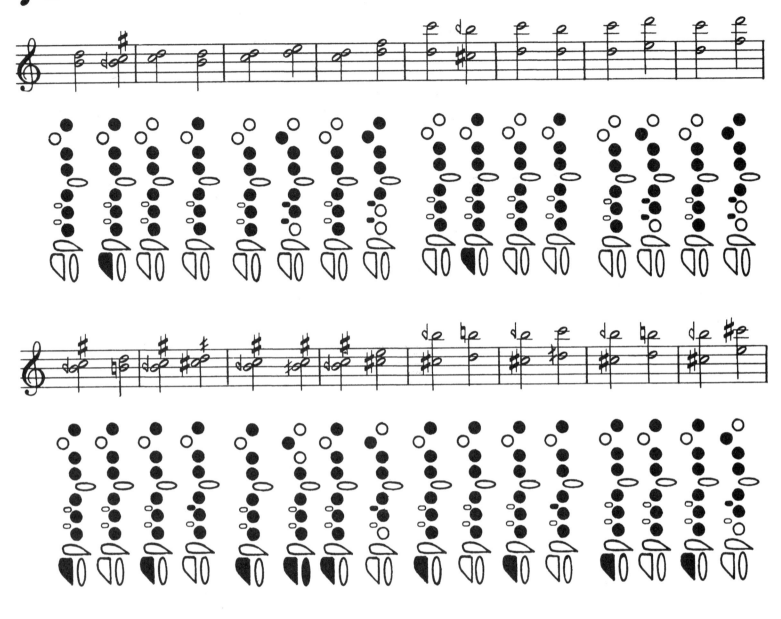

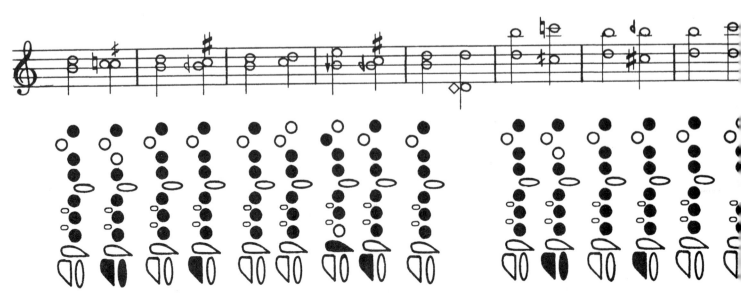

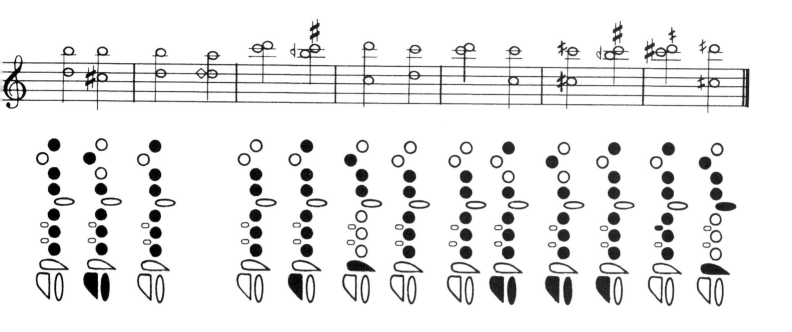

The following exercises involve regular fingerings from the flute's third octave, which produce multiphonics with wide dynamic ranges. Two additional fingerings, acoustically similar to most third octave fingerings are included as well. In exercise N combinations of the first and second partials and of the second and third partials produced by $E\flat^6$, F^6, G^6, A^6, $B\flat^6$, $B\natural^6$ and the two added fingerings are given and explored. Production of these intervals is quite straight-forward, and the practice procedures outlined earlier in this chapter should be followed. The very wide intervals in exercise O, however, have a production technique of their own. After finding the embouchure position for the lower note, keep the jaw in position for the low pitch and stretch the lips far back while greatly increasing the air speed, and the upper note will sound, skipping the pitch normally found between the two notes. This motion is contrary to standard tone production, but is a very good exercise for the strength and flexibility of the lips.

Lastly, exercise P gives the multiphonics produced by the regular fingerings of $E\natural^6$, $F\#^6$ and $A\flat^6$. These intervals differ markedly in timbre from those in exercises N & O, and are quite penetrating.

Exercise N

♩ = 60

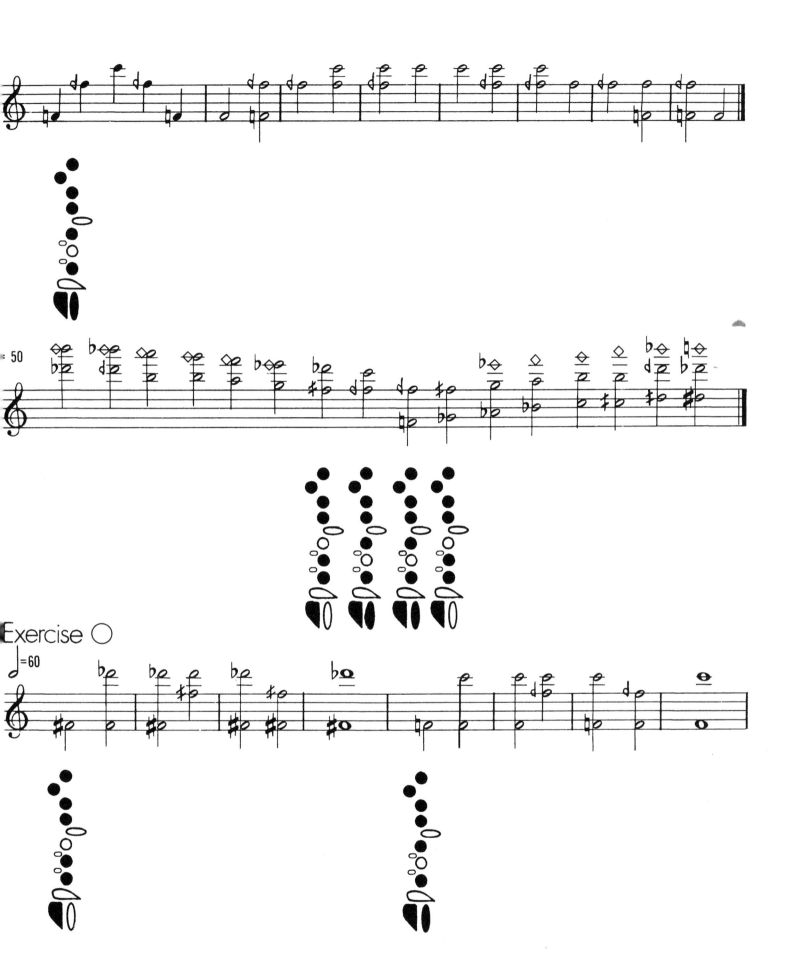

Exercise ○

Exercise P

Exercises Q and R involve more intervals produced by half-holing open-hole keys. These multiphonics are among the most attractive sounding, and can be played with a rich, resonant sonority. Be sure the center-holes are completely open and to tune the throat to the weaker pitch in each case. The last two fingerings in Exercise R each contain several smaller intervals and a larger interval. In playing the large intervals, keep the lips firm and use a strong airstream. The $\mathbf{\textit{ff}}$ dynamic is literal.

Exercise R